MIRACLES:
GOD'S HANDS
AT WORK

JASMINE ANN PHILLIPS

WESTBOW
PRESS
A DIVISION OF THOMAS NELSON

Scriptures taken from the Holy Bible, New International Version®, NIV®.
Copyright © 1973, 1978, 1984, 2011 by Biblica, Inc.™ Used by permission
of Zondervan. All rights reserved worldwide. www.zondervan.com The "NIV"
and "New International Version" are trademarks registered in the United
States Patent and Trademark Office by Biblica, Inc.™ All rights reserved.

WestBow Press books may be ordered through booksellers or by contacting:

WestBow Press
A Division of Thomas Nelson
1663 Liberty Drive
Bloomington, IN 47403
www.westbowpress.com
1-(866) 928-1240

ISBN: 978-1-4497-9124-7 (sc)
ISBN: 978-1-4497-9125-4 (e)

Library of Congress Control Number: 2013906652

Printed in the United States of America.

WestBow Press rev. date: 05/03/2013

TABLE OF CONTENTS

CHAPTER 1

WHERE IT ALL BEGAN

At the age of three (1959), I was hiding under the kitchen table when I heard my mother, Rosa, tell my Aunt Helena, "If it wasn't for her father, I would have left her in the hospital." I cried and was so hurt. I would never forget those words.

Throughout my life my mother always reminded me, "If it wasn't for your father, I would have left you in the hospital." "I never wanted you, your father did." My father died when I was twenty-two years old.

My mother is almost ninety now and lives with my sister Mary, who cares for her, and up until Christmas of 2012 she would remind me, "I never wanted you." It still hurts hearing those words just as much as it did the first time.

I sought counseling in 2009 with counselor Annabella, to help with the hatred I had for my mother. I always felt guilty for hating her because in the Bible it says, " Honor your Father and your Mother," (Exodus 20 NIV) but why didn't she want me or love me?

The counselor helped me to understand it was not my fault that I was born or that my mother did not want me. The counselor advised me I needed to confront my mother; tell her how I felt and how she made me feel all these years, in order to move forward in my life. With that I prayed to God for his guidance. (Proverbs 3:5-6 NIV...Trust in the Lord with all your heart and lean not on your own understanding; in all your ways acknowledge him and he will make your path straight.)

So I prayed for forgiveness for dishonoring my mother. (1 John 1:9 NIV... If we confess our sins, he is faithful and just to forgive us (our) sins, and to cleanse us from all unrighteousness.) It was then peace came upon me.

CHAPTER 2

THE VISION

At the age of seven (1963), while in bed asleep, I felt something nudge me, which caused me to wake up. I looked up and saw the Mother Mary kneeling and floating above me all dressed in white. I got so scared I pulled the covers over my head. I wanted to see if she was still there, so I slowly pulled the covers down and peeked out. She was gone. I put my hand out to see if I could feel anything. I felt nothing. I pulled the covers back over my head and went back to sleep.

When I woke up the next morning I thought, did that really happen? Did I really see the Mother Mary?

Yes I did. I started shaking and was so scared of the thought that the Mother Mary appeared to me. (Job 33:15 NIV... In a dream, in a vision of the night, when deep sleep falls on men as they slumber in their beds.) I wondered Why? Why me? At the same time I felt and knew something different happened to me. I never told anyone because back in those days they would have thought that something was wrong with me.

CHAPTER 3

THE FORGETFUL YEARS

From the ages of five to nine (1961 through 1965), I felt like something bad had happened to me, like I had been sexually abused, and could not recall it. It haunted me for years. I was recently in counseling (2012) for this, in hopes of being able to recall what happened and put my mind at ease. Patten, the counselor, suggested to first talk through it with her, and then try hypnosis, in order to bring it forward. She stated, "Sometimes it does not work, especially if something is very suppressed."

It kept gnawing at me all these years and I felt I needed to know the truth no matter what had happened. I knew I would not be mad or angry. I wanted to know if it happened or not to be able to put my mind at ease, not necessarily to find out who did it.

Then one night I received a phone call from Jimmy, a man I had not seen or spoken to in years, even though we knew each other a long time. I began telling him my story about how I felt something happened to me in my earlier years. He said, "I know what happened and whom it happened with." I asked him to tell me, but he said he could not, and that my counselor had to bring it out of me. He gave me hints, but would not come right out and say it.

I had an appointment with my counselor the next day and told her all of what he said. She stated, "If you believe in your mind that a certain person did something to you, then you will accuse them of something maybe they did not do." She said, "You might confront them and accuse them, and they will defend themselves, and you will feel they are lying and that maybe they did do it." She asked me if it mattered if I found out who did it. I stated, "No, I just need to know if it happened or not so I can have *inner peace*." She stated, "You need to talk with the people closest to you to find answers, but keeping an open mind.

I decided I would call my sister and mother first. After speaking with my sister for a period of time, she could not recall anything out of the ordinary happening to me. Then I spoke with my mother for an extensive period of time and she could not recall anything either. My sister got back on the phone and I thought it was just her and I; was I wrong? Was a spirit present? All of a sudden I started to shake and at the same time I'm yelling to my sister, "I can see it happening, but I cannot see who it is. I feel it, it is more than one." Then I yelled and started to cry. I had this surge or something. Whatever it was it left my body. God had cleansed me and removed the evil spirit that lurked within me. I felt an *inner peace*.

(John 14:27 NIV … Peace I leave with you, my peace I give you. I do not give to you as the world gives. Do not let your hearts be troubled and do not be afraid.) My sister asked me, "Are you okay." I said, "Yes, I don't know what happened, but it is gone." The gnawing feeling of being sexually abused was gone. I was at peace and didn't feel the need to know any more. I told my sister, "I need to get off the phone." I did and just sat there in the chair and prayed to God.

I still had another appointment with my counselor before leaving for Miami, Florida for the Christmas holiday 2012.

When she and I got together I told her what had happened. I told her I felt at peace. She reminded me I had other family members and friends I needed to confront while in Florida, so I would know one way or another if anything really did happen.

While in Florida I still felt the *inner peace* God had planted inside of me. I felt like I did not need to ask anyone anything because I already knew through the *grace* of God. (Ephesians 2:8 NIV... For it is by grace you have been saved, through faith – and this is not from yourselves, it is the gift of God.) I did speak with everyone I felt I needed to while in Florida. Not one person had any idea of anything happening to me.

After returning back to Columbus, Ohio I met with my counselor for one last time. After telling her I still felt at peace and did not have anything to add from the last time we spoke, we decided to close my case. At that very moment the spirit spoke to me and said, "Pregnant." I asked my counselor if they had a good holiday," and she said, "Yes, and did I tell you I was pregnant?" I wanted to say, yes, I know, but instead I said, "No," because she had not told me, the spirit did.

God is *good*. God is *great*. God works in mysterious ways.

Chapter 4

Spiritual Gifts

From the ages of nine through fourteen (1965 through 1970), I attended Catholic school in Queens, New York. It was at that time I started having visions and dreams. I would dream things of the future and they would actually happen. I would hear a soft voice in my ear, which I learned over the years, is the spirit speaking to me. I had no idea what any of these things meant.

During the years in Catholic school I do not remember reading the Bible other than we had to memorize the Ten Commandments (Exodus 20:3-17 NIV...

"You shall have no other gods before me.

"You shall not make for yourself an idol in the form of anything in heaven above or on the earth beneath or in the waters below. You shall not bow down to them or worship them; for I, the Lord your God, am a jealous God, punishing the children for the sin of the fathers to the third and fourth generation of those who hate me, but showing love to a thousand generations of those who love me and keep my commandments.

"You shall not misuse the name of the Lord your God, for the Lord will not hold anyone guiltless who misuses his name.

"Remember the Sabbath day by keeping it holy. Six days you shall labor and do all your work, but the seventh day is a Sabbath to the Lord your God. On it you shall not do any work, neither you, nor your son or daughter, nor your manservant or maidservant, nor your animals, nor the alien within your gates. For in six days the Lord made the heavens and the earth, the sea, and all that is in them, but he rested on the seventh day. Therefore the Lord blessed the Sabbath day and made it holy.

"Honor your father and your mother, so that you may live long in the land the Lord your God is giving you.

"You shall not murder.

"You shall not commit adultery.

"You shall not steal.

"You shall not give false testimony against your neighbor.

"You shall not covet your neighbor's house. You shall not covet your neighbor's wife, or his manservant or maidservant, his ox or donkey, or anything that belongs to your neighbor.")

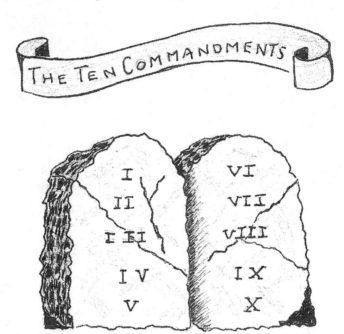

At some point I remember hearing something about gifts from God, *spiritual gifts* (1 Corinthians 12:8-10 NIV..."To one there is given through the Spirit the message of wisdom, to another the message of knowledge by means of the same Spirit, to another faith by the same Spirit, to another gifts of healing by that one Spirit, to another miraculous powers, to another prophecy, to another distinguishing between spirits, to another speaking in different kinds of tongues, and to still another the interpretation of tongues.") and thought, is that what I have? Still not having true understanding and knowledge, I told no one. I was still so afraid whoever I told would think I was crazy.

At this time I also became very rebellious towards my mother due to not understanding why she did not want me. I started doing drugs, (up to the age of seventeen) smoking, drinking, stealing, swearing, having sex and hanging out with the wrong crowd of people. I was on the road to destruction, but God was watching over me (Psalm 121:7 NIV...The Lord will keep you from all harm – he will watch over your life.) because I am here today to tell my story.

At the age of sixteen (1972), my parents moved me to Tampa, Florida to live with my brother. It would be there that for the first time I would tell a friend about these gifts, *spiritual gifts.* (1 Corinthians 12:7-11 NIV) and that I could hear a soft voice, and I knew things of the future both good and bad. As I began to tell her I started to shake. The more I told her, the more I shook, until I almost passed out. I got real scared and felt sick to my stomach. I told no one else.

CHAPTER 5

INFIDELITY

I n 1973, while still living in Florida, I met my future husband Robert. We married in 1974 and have four beautiful children together.

Due to never feeling loved by my mother for the words that would haunt me, "I never wanted you," I never felt loved or wanted by anyone. During the fifteen years of marriage I never felt loved or I belonged, always craving for my mother's love. The road to destruction took another turn. I committed adultery.

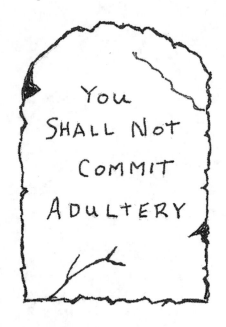

(Exodus 19:14 NIV...You shall not commit adultery.) I knew in my heart what I did was wrong. I felt guilty for what I did. I was out of control and did not know what to do.

The visions, dreams and soft voices continued. On one occasion I told my husband to be careful when he was leaving for work because I had a vision something bad was going to happen. I started that shaking thing again as I told him. He made me aware that day to never tell someone something bad is going to happen.

There were times I could hear my sister's cry in my ear. I would call her and ask her, "What is wrong?" She would say, "How did you know." I would tell her, "I could hear you in my ear." When any of my children would cry as babies I could hear them off in a distance. Even now as adult children I know what is going on before they even call and tell me. Still never telling anyone what I knew inside of me.

Then one day I read somewhere something about God's *gifts* and it had the verse and quote from the Bible, (1 Corinthians 12:7-11 NIV) and I thought, Wow, that is what I have. I put that together with the vision of Mother Mary and felt that *spiritual gifts* is what she delivered to me that night. Still too afraid to tell anyone.

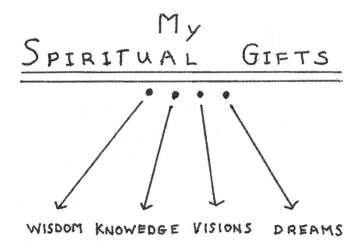

As the years went by I decided to tell my best friend Lizbeth. She asked me if I was *psychic* and I said, "No."

Then she wanted to test me, which lead me to another reason why not to tell anyone. I did not need to be tested. I knew what was true inside of me. What God planted inside of me was for his works.

CHAPTER 6

DESTRUCTIVE YEARS

After divorcing my husband (1994), and while raising our four children, I put myself through college and graduated with a degree in nursing. During that time I met a young man, Joseph, sixteen years younger than me. We lived together for about two years. During that time I demanded we be intimate numerous times in a day. I wanted to be loved so bad and thought that would fulfill the void. It did not. It left me empty and lonely inside.

After him I met another man, William. We lived together for about three years. He had a drug problem and promised he would get help. He never did and became abusive towards me. He would put his hands on me and leave bruises. He would choke me until I passed out. The final straw came when he pushed me into a glass door and spit on me. From the corner of my eye I could see my children watching. I called the police and had him arrested. When he got out of jail I begged him to come back. You ask yourself, "Why?" It's the loneliness, the fear of being alone. (Psalm 121:7 NIV) I never questioned God as to why. Every night I would pray to him to keep me and my children safe. He did.

Then I started having all these strange thoughts of becoming someone's sex slave; being submissive to men. I never knew these things really existed in our world. Then came the computer porn; I was becoming addicted. All because I wanted my mother's love, just to be loved.

I decided to go on line (dating sites) to meet men. I met this one man in particular, Frankie, that I knew was going to turn my world upside down and inside out. That soft voice told me to turn around and run. I did not listen. It would be ten years of pure mental abuse. This man opened my eyes up to a whole other world and that bondage (sex slaves and being submissive to others) really existed. I would scan the sites on the computer and think I wanted someone to hurt me like that. So now the destruction was taking another turn. If I couldn't get the love I needed and wanted one way, I'd get it another way. The affliction of pain.

I was so spiritually connected to this man I could feel his spirit everywhere around me (God was protecting me). What I thought was a good spirit turned out to be an evil spirit. On one occasion when we were together, sitting and talking, I closed my eyes and transformed myself into him. I could not hear anything and I felt like I was floating on air. I brought myself back out of him and just sat there. He still talking and I was thinking to myself, what just happened. Never to do that again.

On the same occasion, as we held each other, I had my eyes closed, I heard this growling sound, (animal like noise) and I opened my eyes and the face I saw on this man was nothing human I had ever seen before. I closed my eyes, let my body go limp and prayed and prayed and prayed to God not to let this creature hurt me. I was scared to death. I waited a long time before opening up my eyes and when I did it was gone. I wanted to get up and run, but I couldn't move my body. I never told anyone, but knew it was not a good thing.

My life was getting more out of control by the minute. I wanted it to stop. I couldn't get it to stop and didn't know how.

Chapter 7

Breaking Point

Then in 2004 I got severely sick. I could not get up out of bed. Could not walk, was in excruciating pain. Could not drive, cook or clean. It took everything I had to just take a shower. I could not even get up to go to work.

I went to Dr. Canon and he told me I was depressed. I said, "No way." I was a nurse. I did not feel depressed (whatever that was). I wanted him to run tests and do lab work. Everything came back normal. I went to another physician for a second opinion and she wanted to put me on antidepressants. I said, "No, I'm not depressed."

She said, "If you aren't going to listen then do not come back." So I went back to my physician and told him I believed in what he told me and I would do whatever he wanted me to do.

This was the worst time in my life and I was at my breaking point. My children and family could not understand what was going on. I felt so all alone and unloved again. When people cannot see your illness or pain they do not believe you to be ill.

BREAKING POINT

I was off work for three months. I was angry at the world. Why was this happening to me. I went through the five stages of grief: Denial, Anger, Bargaining, Depression, Acceptance. I prayed to God asking him, "Why is this happening to me?" even though knowing not to ask God why. When I finally accepted this illness, I knew God gave it to me for a reason.

Everything I went through up to this point God allowed me to have that experience, and I knew it, so I could use it in my daily care of nursing. To have the understanding of other people. and be able to feel and know what they are going through.

Depression doesn't go away, it subsides. It hides itself and when you least expect it, it shows up again. Throughout this time my physician would put me on different antidepressants only to make my symptoms worse, like the feeling of wanting to die, hopelessness and helpless. All during this time I knew God was working through me.

Then one day I woke up and was crying uncontrollably. I couldn't stop crying. I wanted to die. I was trying to take a shower and was hysterical and could not stop crying. I got out of the shower and looked in the mirror and said, "You need help." I got dressed and called 911.

I was admitted to the hospital on the Behavioral Unit. I met with the Psychiatrist the next day and he asked me, "So tell me what is going on in your life?"

I told him of the unhealthy relationship I was in with this man. He said, "You have two choices: you either end it or I will call him and tell him myself." I told him, "I will tell him." I was also started on a new antidepressant.

It was not easy to end the relationship. I became dependent on this man. I prayed to God for guidance. (Proverbs 3:6-6 NIV) Eventually I was able to free myself from him. I tried to be friends, but that is unthinkable, because you will go back to what feels normal even in a bad situation.

Through every experience I never lost my faith. I always prayed to God to keep me safe. He never left my side and was with me every step of the way. (Psalm 121:7 NIV).

CHAPTER 8

KNOWLEDGE AND WISDOM

Throughout my years of nursing, when I was caring for the sick, I could see through my visions (the *spiritual gifts* from God) what was hurting inside of them, (1 Corinthians 12:8-10 NIV) whether it be physical pain, mental anguish or some type of abuse. I was able to use all my God given experiences to be able to feel what people felt and have the knowledge and understanding to comfort them. The more I used my God given gifts, (1 Corinthians 12:8-10 NIV) the stronger the gifts became.

Even to this day I can look at people and through my visions and feel whatever type of disruption is going on inside of them. I can look at people, and through their eyes I can hear them talk to me without them making a sound, and I comfort them. What I used to be so afraid of, I no longer am, because I know they are gifts from God.

In 2011 I met Michael, and I would become very in tune with his spirit, a good spirit. This was the man of my dreams. When we first met and while having dinner I asked him, "Can you really sing?" See, ever since I was a little girl, I always knew the man that sang to me would be the man of my heart. No other man could sing to me up to this point, even though they tried. He said, Yes, I can really sing." I then asked him if he would sing to me and he did.

When I look at this man I could see and feel deep in his soul. There was a lot of hurt, disappointments, pain and anger. I would tell him what I could see and feel about him. As I was telling him these things he would just stare at me. I told him as I have told others, "If what I say is not true then correct me." No one has to this point.

Then one day I got this deep dark feeling inside of me that something was going to happen to him. Remembering what my ex-husband told me, not to express negativity, I said nothing to this man. At five pm that evening I could feel something was happening to him. I started to shake all over. I went to his picture and I felt his pain. I did not want to call him at that time, because I knew he would be driving to work. When I knew his shift was over at work, I texted him telling him to be careful coming home and he texted me back telling me it was too late, he was already in a car accident. He later called me and I told him what time I went to his picture and how I started to shake, and he told me that was the time the accident occurred. He wanted to know how I knew. I told him, "Through my visions."

Upon speaking with my Pastor Suzanne, and informing her of my gifts, she stated to me, "It is one thing to have knowledge, but it is another to have wisdom." I understood what God was telling me through her.

Chapter 9

The Coming of a New Beginning

L ate Spring of 2012, in the candy aisle of the grocery store, (until this day we still laugh and chuckle over it) I ran into Suzanne, whom I hadn't seen in years. We used to attend church together back then. I ask her, "What have you been up to and where are you attending church now a days?" I knew some twenty years ago when I first met her, something *great* would happen between us. She proceeded to tell me. " I am a Minister now and preach in a church in another town." I told her I was looking for a church and asked if I could attend. She said, "Sure." I could feel my spirit jumping and getting excited inside of me. This was the beginning of my transformation to *a new life.*

I went to church that Sunday and I was scared to death. I knew no one and did not know what to do. Had no idea what was about to happen in my life. Everyone smiled and welcomed me with open arms. I knew right away this is where I needed to be and belonged. I prayed to God thanking him for bringing this woman back in my life. The Pastor (my friend) had someone looking out for me and told them, "She would be the one with the lost look on her face." I was lost alright and for many years.

I sat through service, and believe you me, I was a nervous wreck. I could feel God calling me to him. I wanted to get up and run, but my body would not move. After the service, Pastor and I talked for a few minutes and then I left. I felt an excitement inside of me. I began to shake again.

I went a few more Sundays. Then this one Sunday the Pastor and I went to lunch and I told her of my road of destruction. I began to cry. I could feel this heaviness starting to leave me. The more I confessed my sins to her, (1 John l:9 NIV) the lighter I felt inside and I began to shake. I knew inside of me I wanted a new life, but did not know what to do. I told her this and she said,

"Start with prayer." We prayed together right then and there. I told her, "I want to be able to read the Bible and understand it." She said, "Pray over that and start with Matthew."

I did this, plus when I first went to church someone gave me this little devotional book. I put all that together, opened the Bible and began to read. For the first time in my life I was able to understand it. I could not wait to get back to church and tell her. The more I read the Bible the more I could feel the changes inside of me. God was working on me. I was starting to feel loved inside of me.

I met with the Pastor a few more Sundays to talk and each time I had something new inside of me to tell her. I told her that when I opened up my Bible to read now, I understood what it was saying to me. She said, "Great." I said, "I can feel the transformation getting stronger and stronger until one day I knew it happened and told her I was born again."

TRANSFORMATION

My desires to go out and do evil things in the flesh were decreasing. It was the craziest and best thing I had ever experienced in my life. The more I prayed and read His word (the Bible) the more I could feel and see the transformation transpiring. I knew I did not want to go back to the life of destruction.

In September of 2012 I lost my job, went into depression and ended up back in the hospital again. That is where I was given a book on depression written by a woman Minister. I read the book and thought who is this woman. I want more of her knowledge. I then asked my Pastor about her and she knew her name and said, "She also has a television show." When I returned home I found her TV show and at the end of her show it showed she has a website and does medical missions. I was so excited about all of this, and the possibility of going to another country and helping others was always a dream of mine.

Now I was just not reading my Bible daily, I was also listening to her sermons on a daily basis. God was bringing me closer and closer to him. I was beginning to understand him (God) and all that he has done for me; all that he wants to do for me. I joined the church and for the first time in my life I felt loved and belonged somewhere.

I no longer can go out and physically work, but am working for God now on a daily basis. He called me and I obeyed. He has inspired me to write my story. Without God I could not have written my story. With the pain in my hand, to write would have been too difficult. He takes my pain away. (Psalm 30:2 NIV... O Lord my God, I called to you for your help and you healed me.) I have opened up my home to care for people with disabilities and am taking classes to certify in Foster Care Parenting. My loneliness and emptiness are now filled with the joy of God and all his works, which I do on a daily basis. With all my daily readings, devotions and TV sermons, my heart and soul are filled with the Holy Spirit. I feel so rich and blessed. I am involved with my church and do all of what God calls me to do.

I still have a lot to learn. The good road is a narrow road, but it is the benefits of God my father that keeps me on it. I'm living it and loving it daily. Do I still get scared? Yes I do, but I go to the Father and pray to him and he takes my troubles away.

I am living proof that transformations do take place and *spiritual gifts* do exist. If I can do it, so can you. God Bless You!

THE END

Printed in the United States
By Bookmasters